Yes
HOLY SPIRIT

How to live a Spirit-Empowered life every day

GORDON MOORE

Ark House Press
PO Box 1722, Port Orchard, WA 98366 USA
PO Box 1321, Mona Vale NSW 1660 Australia
PO Box 318 334, West Harbour, Auckland 0661 New Zealand
arkhousepress.com

Cataloguing in Publication Data:
Title: Yes Holy Spirit
ISBN: 978-0-9942832-4-5 (pbk.)
Subjects: Christian Living/Holy Spirit/Spiritual Growth
Other Authors/Contributors: Moore, Gordon

Design and layout by initiateagency.com

Contents

We are living in times when it has become almost unfashionable, even unacceptable to encourage the work of the Holy Spirit and supernatural manifestations in the life of the Church.

Incredibly, at the same time, it seems our entire world however is constantly besotted by a desire to experience supernatural phenomena. Every second movie is about spiritual entities - witches, wizards, spells and curses, angels and demons. The hunger to experience God is evident and obvious.

The Church has always meant to be a house filled with the great person of the Holy Spirit empowering believers to do the work of Jesus.

Healing the sick, deliverance from demons, raising the dead, signs and wonders were all part of the new testament experience in the book of Acts. Contrary to some beliefs these have not ceased but continue today – The Holy Spirit is still empowering believers to heal, set free and bring the signs of God to this earth.

As we remain open to the Holy Spirit we will fulfil His greatest work which is to glorify Jesus and point people to Him. No one can be born again except by the Spirit, Jesus said. Thus it becomes imperative that people have a genuine conversion experience where they can declare with complete conviction that they have truly been born again by the Holy Spirit.

I know that Gordon Moore's commitment to building the church, glorifying Jesus Christ, is accomplished through his deep commitment to the Holy Spirit being active in his personal life and the life of the great church he leads. Gordon's treatment of this matter will greatly help the growth and advancement of the church. I know whoever reads this will find themselves travelling deeper into their encounter with God, His Holy Spirit and Jesus Christ the Son.

Dr Phil Pringle, OAM
Founder and President of C3 Church Global

Pentecost is Personal

The Day of Pentecost changed a group of bewildered followers into a band of **SPIRIT EMPOWERED CHURCH BUILDERS**. What happened?

When the Holy Spirit came on the first Day of Pentecost, the disciples, all 120 of them, were filled with the Holy Spirit and began laughing, crying, shaking, falling down, dancing, swaying, singing, preaching and speaking in foreign languages they had never learned. They were seen out in the streets, among their neighbours, empowered by the influence of the Holy Spirit.

That day, 3,000 people believed in Christ and joined the 120 disciples to form the first Church. By the fourth chapter of Acts, another 5,000 men believed, giving an estimated membership of the new church of around 20,000 people (men, women and children).

> *"Many of them which heard the word believed;*
> *and the number of the men was about five thousand."*
> *(Acts 4:4)*

This was no small occurrence. God was establishing His Church with power, persuasion and the supernatural. The impact on Jerusalem was huge, causing concern among the Jewish leaders who banned the preaching and spreading of their message.

> *'And when they had brought them, they set them before the council,*
> *and the high priest asked them, saying, "Did not we strictly*
> *command you that you should not teach in this name? And, behold,*
> *you have filled Jerusalem with your doctrine, and intend to bring this*
> *man's blood upon us."*
> *Then Peter and the other apostles answered and said,*
> *We ought to obey God rather than men.'*
> *(Acts 5:27-29)*

You're exaggerating the scene aren't you? Well, not according to what the onlookers saw and supposed as a result of all the commotion:

> *"And they were all astounded and perplexed,*
> *saying to one another, "What could this be?"*
> *But some sneered and said, "They are full of new wine!"*
> *(Acts 2:12-13)*
> *"What could this be?" They exclaimed!*

This event was so different, extraordinary and confronting compared to anything that had occurred before in Jewish religious history. There was no frame of reference for it, no precedence, no understanding.

"So Peter, emboldened and inspired by the Holy Spirit, stood up and explained,
> *"These are not drunk as you suppose...but THIS IS THAT which*
> *was spoken by the prophet Joel..." (Acts 2:15-16)*

But wait a minute, Joel didn't mention 'tongues' specifically, did he? No.
   But Peter did!

Peter was preaching by 'divine inspiration' which enabled him to interpret, explain and contextualize the prophecy of Joel. 'Scripture interpreting Scripture'!
Why do 'strange things' happen like this?

Introduction

A study of the history of revivals and moves of God reveal the following characteristics:

1 . Any genuine move of the Holy Spirit, like the Day of Pentecost, is **sovereign and supernatural**.[1]

Such revivals are not from man, by man, or maintained by man. They are beyond human initiation, comprehension, evaluation, expectation and thinking.

When the Holy Spirit's power comes, physicality and human understanding are superseded!

2 . Such moves of the Holy Spirit are **so deep and profound** that emotions and human physicality go into overload, because humanity simply cannot cope with the overwhelming presence and power of God. Physical and emotional 'extremes' are simply the reality of 'human overload'.

3 . Such moves of the Holy Spirit reveal that **God does not respect, nor is He restricted by, any religious belief system, conditions or limitations.**

Every move of God in history is associated with expressions, forms and results that always contradict and challenge accepted religious conventions and practices.

The Holy Spirit is no gentleman. Human convention, rules, manners and etiquette do not apply!
When God decides it's time… **IT'S TIME!**

---

1. *Every revival, or move of the Holy Spirit, has a specific duration and restores an aspect of truth and experience that has been lost to the Church through history.*

The true essence of Christianity is not a man-centred, man derived, or man initiated activity…

Christianity is all about the
Holy Spirit of God
Acting sovereignly and redemptively
In order to fulfill the will and
Purposes of God!

Easter, 6 April 1968

When the Holy Spirit first visited me in 1968, I was part of an Easter Baptist Youth Camp in Hastings, New Zealand. I responded to the altar call on the Sunday evening and received Christ as my personal Saviour and Lord.

After the meeting, I was invited to a prayer meeting where I received prayer to 'receive the Holy Spirit'.

As the leaders placed their hands on my head, I immediately began to shake, feel and appear intoxicated. People who witnessed this experience happening to me said that I was loud and slurred in speech – 'drunk and intoxicated'. Yet I had not touched any alcohol or intoxicating substance. I was at a Baptist youth camp!

I began to speak fluently in an unknown language that I had never learned; falling down physically as I did so and experiencing an overwhelming sense of the presence of God.

For weeks after this experience, every time I began to speak in tongues, whether in public or private, I became immediately 'intoxicated' and would often fall down into a trance-like state of overwhelming joy and peace.

As a result of this dramatic experience, which lasted for weeks, I possessed an instant hunger to know God, His Word and the presence of the Holy Spirit. I began to devour the Bible; reading chapter after chapter, often falling asleep late at night with my face buried in the pages of my Bible.

The speech impediment that I had since childhood, which resulted in me being sent to speech classes at school, was instantly healed.

This shy sixteen year old was inhibited no longer!

A new boldness, confidence and articulation filled my life. I was instantly able to speak, communicate and preach with impact beyond my years of experience and knowledge.

I discovered that the Scripture is true when it declares, *"You shall receive **power** when the Holy Spirit comes on you and you shall **be my witnesses.**" (Acts 1:8)*

Over the last 45 years since that time, I have had my experience questioned, and sometimes disapproved of by the supposed 'experts'! I have also witnessed some extremes and excesses not worthy of mention.

But this one thing I know... I have experienced my personal Pentecost!

The Holy Spirit visited me just like He visited the disciples in the Acts of the Apostles 2,000 years ago!

My life has been an adventure from that very moment.

YES, HOLY SPIRIT!

Life has not always been smooth sailing and I have had moments of challenge along the way as I have endeavoured to live out my faith. However, I have always possessed a strong sense of an inner awareness and a sensitivity to the presence, promptings and leadings of the Holy Spirit. **He has always been there**!

'I will never leave you, nor forsake you.
So that we may boldly say, The Lord is my helper,
and I will not fear what man shall do to me.'
(Heb 13:5-6)

I wouldn't trade the Holy Spirit's baptism, presence and power in my life for any morsel of human dignity, philosophy or religion!

I have experienced my personal Pentecost! I'm unashamed of it and have spent my life helping others discover the life changing power of the Holy Spirit's presence.

What is the Purpose of a Personal Pentecost?

Since those early, heady days, I have come to discover more about the purpose and meaning of this extraordinary experience.

I have found that there are basically **four central purposes** of the Baptism of the Holy Spirit:

1 . To EMPOWER us to be WITNESSES of Christ
"But ye shall receive power,
after that the Holy Ghost is come upon you:
and ye shall be witnesses unto me." (Acts 1:8)

2. To RELEASE the SUPERNATURAL in our lives
"God also bearing them witness,
both with signs and wonders,
and with various miracles,
and gifts of the Holy Spirit." (Heb 2:4)

3. To SET US FREE FROM OURSELVES to BE
OURSELVES - to discover our best life!
"Now the Lord is that Spirit:
and where the Spirit of the Lord is, there is liberty (freedom)."
(2Cor 3:17)

4. To EQUIP us with GIFTS FOR SERVICE for the
BUILDING UP OF THE CHURCH
"Now to each one the manifestation of the Spirit
is given for the common good...
...All these are the work of one and the same Spirit,
and He gives them to each one, just as He determines."
(1Cor 12:7,11)

CHAPTER ONE

Who Is The Holy Spirit?

The Holy Spirit is a divine, spiritual being. He is the third person of the Eternal Godhead.

"For there are three that bear record in heaven,
the Father, the Word, and the Holy Spirit:
and these three are one."
1 Jn 5:7

The Holy Spirit is equal and identical to the Father and the Son in every divine essence, attribute, characteristic and power, and yet an individual, divine person.

The Holy Spirit has willingly submitted to the Father and the Son, the Lord Jesus Christ, to be sent to earth as the agent of salvation for mankind, and to be the Comforter and Guide to all believers.

"But the Comforter, who is the Holy Spirit,
whom the Father will send in my name,
He will teach you all things..."
(Jn 14:26)

The Holy Spirit is therefore active and present in the lives of every human being. He is sent by God to bring a conviction and an awareness of Christ to every person.

'It is expedient for you that I go away:
for if I go not away, the Comforter will not come unto you;

but if I depart, I will send Him unto you.
And when He is come, He will convict the world of sin,
and of righteousness, and of judgment:
Of sin, because they believe not on me;
Of righteousness, because I go to my Father, and you see me no
more;
Of judgment, because the prince of this world is judged.'
(Jn 16:6-11)

Once we receive Christ through the spiritual new birth, the Holy Spirit continues His work in every believer of developing a sanctified life of faith, holiness and service for Christ.

It is through the work of the Holy Spirit that every person is able to hear the Gospel and discover forgiveness, salvation and a new life in Christ. The Holy Spirit accomplishes this work through the Church by empowering, gifting and mobilising believers to be witnesses of Christ.

The focus of the Christian life, therefore, is receiving and learning to recognise the presence of the Holy Spirit so we can hear His voice in our hearts and respond to the will of Christ.

"But the anointing which you have received of Him abides in you,
and you need not that any man teach you:
but as the same anointing teaches you of all things, and is truth, and
is no lie, and even as it has taught you, you shall abide in Him."
(1Jn 2:27)

CHAPTER TWO

Entrance Into the Supernatural

The Christian life is a **spiritual,** or **supernatural experience.**

The Christian life cannot be experienced and lived out on human terms, or by natural means.

It must by nature be **entered into supernaturally** and be **continued supernaturally**, through the **presence** and **power** of the **Holy Spirit.**

> *"But the natural man does not receive the things of the Spirit of God,*
> *for they are foolishness to him nor can he know them,*
> *because they are spiritually discerned."*
> *(1 Cor 2:14)*

The apostle Paul was concerned for the Galatians, who had begun their Christian experience supernaturally but had reverted to religious laws and rules, which made their faith natural, or human, rather than supernatural.

> *"Are you so foolish and so senseless and so silly?*
> *Having begun [your new life spiritually] with the [Holy] Spirit,*
> *are you now reaching perfection [by dependence] on the flesh?"*
> *(Gal 3:3) AMP*

John captures the essence of the Christian life in his gospel when he declared that the Christian life is entered into by a **'supernatural rebirth'** through the work of the Holy Spirit.

"Who were born, not of blood, nor of the will of the flesh,
nor of the will of man, but of God." (Jn 1:13)

Just like the game of Monopoly, where to start playing you must throw a double six on the die, so to start the Christian life you **MUST** be **'born of God'.**

"Unless one is born again
he cannot see the kingdom of God…
…unless one is born of water and the Spirit
he cannot enter the Kingdom of God." (Jn 3:3,5)

These statements by Jesus leave us in **no doubt: -**

STEP ONE IN THE CHRISTIAN LIFE
IS THE 'NEW BIRTH'

The new birth is a marvel, a miracle that cannot be underestimated.

The new birth endows the new believer with **two supernatural gifts from God**:

1 . The '**Gift of Revelation'**
The believer is gifted with the ability to **'see the Kingdom'** - the grace **to perceive, understand and know** spiritual truth and realities promised by God.

"But the anointing which you have received
from Him abides in you,
and you do not need anyone to teach you;
but the same anointing teaches you
concerning all things, and is true…" (1Jn 2:27)

This gift of revelation is the foundation of Christian faith, a faith based on revelation knowledge of God's word.

2. The '**Gift of Entrance**'
The believer is gifted with the ability to **'enter the Kingdom'** - the grace to actually **know by personal experience** the spiritual truth and realities promised by God.

> "And my speech and my preaching
> were not with persuasive words of human wisdom,
> but in demonstration of the Spirit and of power,
> that your faith should not be in the wisdom of men
> but in the power of God." (1 Cor 2:4-5)

A Historical view

The way the Pietists, in the 1600s, viewed the salvation experience is helpful. They recognized that a person was saved through **a conscious, personal experience of the new birth.**

> "But as many as received Him,
> to them He gave the power to become children of God,
> to those who believe in His Name." (Jn 1:12)

THE **NEW BIRTH** IS A **CONSCIOUS**, **PERSONAL**,
LIFE TRANSFORMING EXPERIENCE

> "If anyone is in Christ, he is a new creation,
> old things have passed away,
> behold all things have become new." (2 Cor 5:17)

The nature of the New Birth experience

The Scriptures present the new birth experience as having the following three characteristics:

1. "BORN OF THE SPIRIT"
The phrase 'born of the Spirit' can be more correctly rephrased **"born from above"** (margin notes, Holman Bible), that is, **'from heaven'**.

The new birth instantly creates a **'spiritual',** or **'heavenly person'.**

"But he who is spiritual..." (1Cor 2:14)

That is, **Spiritually...**

- orientated
- minded
- directed
- influenced
- aware
- empowered

2. "BORN OF THE SEED"
"Having been born again,
not of corruptible seed, but of incorruptible,
through the Word of God which lives and abides forever." (1Pet 2:23)

The Greek word for "seed" here is "spora" (G4701 - Strongs), which literally means "a sowing".

This is referring to the sowing of **'God's DNA'**, or the **nature of God** into the very being: the heart, soul and mind, of the newly born Christian through the Word of God.

The Holy Spirit deposits the **'seed of His Word'** into our hearts at New Birth and as a result of this sowing:

- **growth** will occur
- **increase** will occur
- the **'DNA (or nature) of God'** will emerge
- **progress** will appear
- **freedom** will be experienced
- a **new life of pleasing God** will develop

"Whoever is born of God does not practice sin,
for His seed remains in him, and he cannot
("deliberately, knowingly and habitually")

sin, because he is born of God." (1Jn. 3:9, [AMP]

3. "BORN OF FAITH"
*"Whoever is **born of God overcomes the world:** and this is **the victory** that overcomes the world, even **our faith.**" (1Jn 5:4)*

Every newborn Christian is imparted with a **'faith Spirit' from God that produces an empowered, overcoming, victorious, and successful life.**

Nothing can hold back the born again, child of God!

Not the devil, not the world, not any human problem... **nothing!**

> THE NEW CHRISTIAN IS BORN INTO
> THE SUPERNATURAL ORDER OF GOD

The new Christian is instantly **empowered by the Holy Spirit** to:
* supersede
* overcome
* succeed
* prosper
* rule
* conquer
* change things

> *"For whatsoever is born of God **overcomes** the world: and this is the **victory** that overcomes the world, even our faith." (1Jn 5:4)*

CHAPTER THREE

The Baptism in the Holy Spirit

The Holy Spirit's two main projects in the world are to:

a. "**Glorify Christ**"

> *"Howbeit when He, the Spirit of Truth, is come,*
> *He will guide you into all truth:*
> *for He shall not speak of himself;*
> *but whatsoever He shall hear, that shall he speak:*
> *and He will show you things to come*
> *He shall glorify me:*
> *for He shall receive of mine, and shall show it unto you."*
> *(Jn 16:13-15)*

And to:

b. "**Empower believers**"

The Holy Spirit empowers us by:

i. The establishing of an '**EMPOWERED INTERNAL LIFE OF GODLINESS**'

ii. The establishing of an '**EMPOWERED EXTERNAL LIFE OF MINISTRY AND SERVICE**'

The '**empowered internal life of Godliness**' is the new life that the Holy Spirit creates in the new believer, which causes growth in Godly character and holiness.

> *"For it is God who works in you*
> *both to will and to do of His good pleasure." (Phil 2:13)*

What does an 'empowered external life of ministry and service' look like?

> *"You shall receive power when the Holy Spirit comes on you*
> *And you shall be witnesses unto me." (Acts 1:8)*

1. "YOU SHALL RECEIVE POWER"

When the Holy Spirit comes He always comes in the:

a. **"Power Of His Holiness"** - purity, cleansing, genuineness and truth

* There is power in Holiness (Ps 47:8)
'Holiness' is not a religious, ceremonial practice of 'rule keeping'

"HOLINESS IS THE RESURRECTION POWER OF GOD AT WORK IN THE BELIEVER PRODUCING A 'GODLY LIFE' - A LIFE PLEASING TO GOD!"

> *"And declared to be the Son of God with power,*
> *according to the spirit of holiness,*
> *by the resurrection from the dead:*
> *By whom we have received grace and apostleship,*
> *for obedience to the faith among all nations, for His name:*
> *Among whom are ye also the called of Jesus Christ."*
> *(Rom 1:3)*

*There is beauty in Holiness

> *"Give unto the LORD the glory due unto his name;*
> *worship the LORD in the beauty of holiness."(Ps 29:2)*

Holiness is attractive, ideal, perfect; it draws people in.
 God's Holiness draws us in. Holiness creates willingness and power in our lives

"Your people shall be willing in the day of Your power,
in the beauties of holiness from the womb of the morning."
Ps 110:3

"HOLINESS IS THE RESURRECTION POWER OF
GOD AT WORK IN THE BELIEVER PRODUCING AN
ATTRACTIVE LIFE TO GOD."

---

b. **"Power Of His Creativity"** - change, renewal and restoration

We are **changed instantly** when we are born again...then we are **changed progressively** "day by day"...

"For which cause we faint not;
but though our outward man perish,
yet the inward man is renewed day by day." (2Cor 4:16)

...and

"...from one degree (level) of glory to the next
degree (level) of glory" (2Cor 3:18)

"For we are His workmanship,
created in Christ Jesus unto good works,
which God hath before ordained that we
should walk in them." (Eph 2:10)

c. **"Power Of His Endowment"** - empowered, equipped and set up by the Holy Spirit for success, victory and our best life possible!

The Holy Spirit's giftings are always in power! They create faith and confidence.

"And my speech and my preaching
was not with enticing words of man's wisdom,

but in demonstration of the Spirit and of power:
That your faith should not stand in the wisdom of men,
but in the power of God." (1 Cor 2:4-5)

2. "YOU SHALL BE"
The Holy Spirit always makes us, shifts us and creates us **TO BE** a new person, a better person and to live and exist in a new dimension and level of 'faith, hope and love'.

Our best life!

"But BE filled with the Holy Spirit." (Eph 5:18), is literally in the **'present, continuous tense'** (Vines Dictionary), meaning **"BE BEING FILLED"**, or *"Ever be filled"* (AMPLIFIED Bible)

The idea here is not the experience alone but rather the **constant mode**, or **state of being** as a believer.

> *"...He gave them the **POWER TO BECOME** the children of God." (Jn 1:12)*

"We're **human 'BEINGS'** not human 'DOINGS'!

It's not what we achieve or possess along the journey of life that counts - it's **WHO WE BECOME** that matters to God.

> *"In Him we live and move and have our **BEING**." (Acts 17:28)*

3. "YOU SHALL BE MY WITNESSES"
The transforming power of the Holy Spirit CREATES a living witness and testimony of the love and grace of God for all to see.

We become 'GOD'S STORY' in this world.

We are 'WRITTEN BY GOD'S HAND'.

We are 'HIS LETTER', personally written by the power of the Holy Spirit.

> *"You show and make obvious that you*
> *are a **letter** from Christ delivered by us,*
> *not written with ink but with [the] **Spirit of [the] living***
> ***God**, not on tablets of stone but on tablets of **human hearts**."*
> *(2 Cor 3:3) (Amplified Bible)*

CHAPTER FOUR

Speaking in Tongues and the Supernatural Life

The gift of speaking in tongues, or speaking in foreign languages, is a much misunderstood and can often be a maligned endowment of God's grace.

But what exactly is 'speaking in tongues'?

The best way to answer this frequently asked question is to consider the **abilities** that speaking in tongues provides the spirit filled believer:

1. SPEAKING TO GOD

"For one who speaks in an [unknown] tongue (language) ***speaks*** *not to men but* ***TO GOD***.."*
(1Cor 14:2)

The most important thing to note is **the direction** of speaking in tongues, that is, speaking in tongues is "**to God**". This marvellous gift from God is essentially a '**gift of personal and devotional prayer**'.

Why then is speaking in tongues so important for the believer?

Because the one who speaks in tongues is **directly communicating with God and encouraging their own faith**.

This is a special gift indeed!

Prophecy, on the other hand, is unable to be used in private - because I cannot prophecy to myself!

"For if I pray in an [unknown] tongue (language),
my spirit [by the Holy Spirit within me] prays...
(1Cor 14:14) (Amplified Bible)

The exercising of Speaking in Tongues engages my spirit with the Spirit of God

*"Likewise **the Spirit also helps our infirmities**.*
For we do not know what we should pray for as we ought,
*but the **Spirit Himself** makes **intercession for us***
with groanings which cannot be uttered."(Rom 8:26)

2. SPEAKING MYSTERIES

*"... in spirit He **SPEAKS MYSTERIES.**" (1Cor 14:2)*

The **Amplified Bible** gives a clearer translation of this verse:

"...for no one understands or catches His meaning,
*because in the [Holy] Spirit he **utters secret truths and***
***hidden things** [not obvious to the understanding]."*

Thayer explains these mysteries as "hidden things, secrets and mysteries". His interpretation has the idea of the "secret will of God" which is revealed in a vision or a dream".

There is a direct connection between Speaking in Tongues and the supernatural language of the Holy Spirit - visions and dreams.

The Amplified and the Analytical-literal translations are clear in their distinction that 'Speaking in Tongues' is "*in the Holy Spirit*", that is, 'Speaking in Tongues' is a **supernatural phenomena and capability** that occurs in the human spirit of those who are baptized in the Holy Spirit.

The gift of Speaking in Tongues is the key to enabling the believer to be **in tune** with, and **capable of understanding** supernatural things.

*"God has **revealed** them to us by His Spirit;*
for the Spirit searches all things, yes, the deep things of God."
(1Cor 2:10)

"For who among men knows the things of a man
except the spirit of man within him?
So also no one knows the things of God
except the Spirit of God." (1Cor 2:11)

3. SPEAKING IN TONGUES PERSONALLY BUILDS UP

*"The one speaking in a tongues **BUILDS HIMSELF UP…"***
1Cor 14:4

The gift of Speaking in Tongues is for every believer, because every believer needs this **ability of self-edification**.

This is why Paul exclaimed; *"I wish that all of you spoke in tongues!"* (1Cor 14:5)

The Strongs Concordance defines edifying, or building self up as; *"to be **a house builder**, that is, **construct** or (figuratively) **confirm**, **edify** and **embolden**." (Strongs -G3618)*
The idea of the word 'edify' here is to be strong enough and equipped enough personally to be a **positive**, **corporate influence**, that is, edification is not just for self, but also for the Church!

*"But you shall **receive power***
when the Holy Spirit has come upon you,
*and you shall **be My witnesses***

both in Jerusalem and all Judea and Samaria
and to the ends of the earth." (Acts 1:8)

Speaking in Tongues is the 'best gift' **for the individual
believer** because it encourages the individual believer, while
prophecy is the 'best gift' for the Church because it encourages
the whole Church (1Cor 14:4).

Parham - the 'Father of Pentecost'

Parham and the early Pentecostals understood that the Baptism
in the Holy Spirit and Speaking in Tongues were not just for
the personal gratification of Christians, but rather, a **gift of
power** to raise up a **company** (the Church) of **encouraged,
gifted, victorious** and **supernatural Church builders**!

The 'Classical Pentecostal' position on Tongues, being "**THE
evidence**" came later, and forced men such as F.F. Bosworth,
Parham and Seymour's disciples, to leave their associations
over the issue.

Bosworth's concern was that a focusing on Speaking in
Tongues would lead Christians away from the whole point of
the Baptism in the Holy Spirit: **POWER!**

The early Pentecostals were concerned about the possible
advent of a powerless, tongue-speaking Christian.

The central purpose of the Baptism in the Holy Spirit is to
produce a **spiritual, or supernatural Church** present in a
natural and physical world that will accomplish God's purpose
and work in the earth.

Un-edified, unequipped, unspiritual and powerless
Christians never build the House of God!

"Even so you, since you are zealots of spiritual things,
seek to build up the church, *in order that you may abound."*

(1Cor 14:12)

The Amplified Bible rendering of this verse is helpful:

> *"So it is with yourselves; since you are so eager and ambitious to possess spiritual endowments and manifestations of the [Holy] Spirit, **[concentrate on] striving to excel and to abound [in them] in ways that will build up the church."***
> *(1Cor 14:12) – Amplified Bible*

Jude, in his Epistle, also refers to the need to be **constantly building oneself up** as a believer.

His language is the same as the Apostle Paul and is obviously referring to the power of Speaking in Tongues:

> *"**Building up yourselves** in your most holy faith, **praying in the Holy Spirit**." (Jude 1:20)*

"*Building up yourselves in your most holy faith...*" refers to the need for **personal edification,** as in 1Cor 14:4, which refers to those believers who speak in tongues as "*house builders*", or church builders!

"*Praying in the Holy Spirit*" is the same language and idea as 1Cor 14:14 and is directly referring to the gift of speaking in tongues - a great gift for personal encouragement, building up and strengthening of believers.

CHAPTER FIVE

The Language of the Spirit

"And it shall come to pass afterward
That I will pour out My Spirit on all flesh;
*Your sons and your daughters shall **prophesy**,*
*Your old men shall **dream dreams**,*
*Your young men shall **see visions**." (Jl 2:28)*

"And they were all filled with the Holy Spirit
*and began to **speak** with other tongues,*
*as the Spirit gave them **utterance**." (Acts 2:4)*

When Peter stood on the Day of Pentecost, he was declaring and directly linking **TONGUES** and **PROPHECY, DREAMS** and **VISIONS** as the **LANGUAGE OF THE SPIRIT!** ***"This is what was spoken through the prophet Joel!"*** *Acts 2:16*

When a child is born it begins to learn the language of the human world. Without language we can't function properly. We need to understand, comprehend and communicate to navigate through human life and society.

The same is true in the supernatural life.

Speaking in Tongues is the gateway, the catalyst into a whole new world – the world of the supernatural.

Speaking in Tongues equips us to converse more fully in the language of the Spirit.

*"For if I pray in an unknown tongue **my spirit**
(by the Holy Spirit within me) prays."*
(1 Cor 14:14)

*"He who speaks in a tongue **SPEAKS TO GOD**."*
(1 Cor 14:2)

*"**Spirit** can only be **known by spirit** –*
***God's Spirit** and our **spirits** in **open communion**."*
(1 Cor 2:14) (Message Bible)

TO COMMUNICATE IN THE SPIRIT WE MUST USE
SUPERNATURAL LANGUAGE

---

*"We also **speak these things**,*
not in words taught by human wisdom,
*but in those **taught by the Spirit**,*
***explaining spiritual things to spiritual people**."*
(1 Cor 2:13)

To communicate in the supernatural, or Spirit, we must use and understand the supernatural language of tongues, prophecy, dreams and visions:

TONGUES
PROPHECY
DREAMS
VISIONS

⟫⟫→

"PICTURES ON THE INSIDE" (REVELATION)

Tongues = "From me"
Prophecy = "To me"
Dreams = "In me"
Visions = "For me"

38

SPIRITUAL DREAMS

There are five kinds of Dreams:

1. Usually at night, or in our **'subconscious'**, can be termed **'day dreaming'**

2. **'Nightmares'** – vivid fears relived in our sleep.

3. **'Natural dreams'** – 'sorting and filing' of our fears, needs, desires and passions

4. **'Spiritual or Prophetic Dreams'**
   For example, Joseph (Gen 37:5) and Paul (Acts 16:9)

5. **'Life Dreams'**
   These dreams are the **constant pictures we see on the inside**, in our hearts and minds.

They are so powerful because we subconsciously live out our 'dream' (what we see!)

What do you see?

VISIONS

A vision is what we see either internally or externally by Divine and **immediate inspiration**.

Receiving a vision is usually associated with **an intentional seeking of God** – unlike dreams, which are often unconscious and unintentional.

For example, the apostle Peter saw a vision while he was on a roof top praying and seeking God (Acts 10:9-16)

The prophet Habakkuk shares how he came to see visions.

He declares, *"I will stand..."* (Hab 2:1), referring to the **positive positioning** we need to take in order to receive visions from God.

Habakkuk received visions in the context of his *"sentry, post, duty, office"* (*Strongs*- G4931) that is *"on my watch"*. This language conveys the idea of **watchfulness**, of being alert and exercising carefulness so as to see and hear what God is saying.

"... and set myself..." comes from the word meaning to *'offer or present self'* (Strongs- H3320) to God.

It is from this position that Habakkuk would *"watch to see..."*

Hearing from God is about being able to **receive God's dreams, visions and pictures**.

He has positioned himself to hear.

The prophet Habakkuk had placed himself in a **teachable position**. He was ready to respond to God's instruction, reproof and correction.

The exercise of speaking in tongues tunes our hearts and minds with the Holy Spirit's frequency to receive God's dreams, visions and pictures.

"For as many as are led by the Spirit of God,
They are the sons of God" (Rom 8:14)

CHAPTER SIX

"The Anointing of the Spirit"

"The Spirit of the Lord is upon me **BECAUSE HE HAS ANOINTED ME…"** *(Luke 4:18)*

Understanding the difference between being **baptised, filled and anointed** in the Holy Spirit is important because they are different levels of encountering the Holy Spirit in our lives.

We are **'baptised'** the **FIRST TIME** the Holy Spirit comes upon us

We are **'filled' EVERY TIME** the Holy Spirit comes upon us

We are **'anointed' FOR A TIME (and purpose)** by the Holy Spirit

When we understand **Christ's purpose,** we understand the **purpose of our anointing**.

Jesus spoke twice about the church:

Matt 18:17 – we are to **maintain the unity of the Church**

"Making every effort to keep the unity of the Spirit in the bond of peace." (Eph 4:3)

Matt 16:18 – we are to **build the church**

*"To equip the saints for the work of ministry,
that is, to **build up** the body of Christ." (Eph 4:12)*

We are anointed, therefore, to fulfill these two central purposes of Christ.

It is also very significant that the coming of the Holy Spirit on the Day of Pentecost was the birthing of the Church in power – nothing has changed!

There is a definite link between the coming of the Spirit and building the Church.

The Church is birthed, built and grown by a **company of anointed, gifted and spirit-empowered believers**

*"Because you have been **built** on the foundation
of the apostles and prophets,
with Christ Jesus himself as the cornerstone.
In him the whole building, being **joined together**,
grows into a holy temple in the Lord,
In whom you also are being **built together**
into a dwelling place of God in the Spirit." (Eph 2:20-22)*

The Holy Spirit's power, anointing and giftings are **for the building of the Church**.

*"Since you are zealous in matters of the Spirit,
seek to excel in building up the church." (1Cor 14:12)*

*"A manifestation of the Spirit is given to each person
to **produce what is beneficial**." (1Cor 12:7)*

*"But you shall **receive power**
when the Holy Spirit comes upon you
and you will be **witnesses** unto me…" (Acts1:8)*

WE MUST FIND OUR 'BECAUSE'...

Jesus said...

> *"The Spirit has anointed me* **because...He has anointed me to preach**..." *(Lk 4:18)*

Jesus' 'because' was to preach...

What is your 'BECAUSE'?

You may be **'Baptised** in the Holy Spirit'...but are you **'being filled'**?

You may be ...'being filled'...but are you **'ANOINTED'**?

What is your **'BECAUSE'**?

'BECAUSE'...HE HAS ANOINTED YOU...
Rom 12:6-8
1. ***To Preach?***
2. ***To Serve?***
3. ***To Teach?***
4. ***To Exhort?***
5. ***To Give?***
6. ***To Lead?***
7. ***To Show Mercy?***

> *"So Samuel took the* **horn of oil**, **anointed him** *in the presence of his brothers, and the* **Spirit of the Lord came mightily upon David** *from that day forward." (1Sam 16:13)*

When Samuel came to anoint one of Jesses' sons to be king, it was obviously Eliab because he was the eldest and a good looking, talented and a soldier in Saul's army....

...BUT HE WAS NOT ANOINTED!

And so were all the seven sons of Jesse present before the prophet.

They were all gifted, all believers and all fine young men...

...BUT NOT ONE WAS ANOINTED BY THE LORD!

"Are all your sons here, Jesse?" asked Samuel.

"There is yet the youngest." Jesse said.

"Jesse sent and brought him...The Lord said to Samuel, 'Arise, **anoint him**; **this is he**.'"

It is very important to understand **how the anointing works.**

God does not by-pass His 'chain of command'. The anointing doesn't just happen!

The anointing is imparted through an **anointed person**

> *"Therefore I put you in remembrance*
> *that you stir up the gift of God,*
> *which is in you by the laying on of my hands." (2 Tim 1:6)*

It is possible to be baptised and filled anywhere, anytime, through 'anyone'.

But 'the anointing' is another matter.

The anointing comes to us, just like David, through the hand of **an anointed** leader and in the "**presence of our brothers**", who are to be witnesses.

We discover 'our anointing' in the presence of our church family.

We find our 'because' **IN OUR CHURCH FAMILY**. That's how the Holy Spirit works!

> *"And **God has set some in the church**,*
> *first apostles, secondarily prophets, thirdly teachers,*
> *after that miracles, then gifts of healings, helps,*
> *governments, diversities of tongues." (1Cor 12:28)*

The baptism and fillings of the Spirit has to do with **EMPOWERMENT.**

The anointing of the Spirit has to do with PURPOSE.

CHAPTER SEVEN

The Leading of the Holy Spirit

The Holy Spirit has been sent to be our **guide**.

> *"Howbeit when He, the Spirit of Truth, is come,*
> *He will **guide you** into all truth:*
> *for He shall not speak of Himself;*
> *but whatsoever He shall hear, that shall He speak:*
> *and He will **show you** things to come."*
> *(Jn 16:13)*

God has GONE TO GREAT LENGTHS to make guiding and leading us possible.

But we have a problem...**US!**

We have a number of factors conspiring against us **SO THAT WE CANNOT HEAR THE HOLY SPIRIT!**

For example:

The Devil speaks his message to us

> *"But if our gospel be hid, it is hid to them that are **lost**:*
> *In whom the **god of this world has blinded the minds**
> ***of them which believe not**,*
> *lest the light of the glorious gospel of Christ*
> *who is the image of God, should shine unto them."*
> *(2Cor 4:3-4)*

Our own Sin deafens us

> *"Behold, the LORD'S hand is not shortened,*
> *that it cannot save;*
> *neither His ear heavy, that it cannot hear:*
> *But **your iniquities have separated you from your***
> ***God,***
> *and **your sins have hid His face from you, so that***
> ***he will not hear**." (Is 59:1-2)*

> *"And this is the condemnation,*
> *that light is come into the world,*
> *and **men loved darkness rather than light,***
> ***because their deeds were evil**.*
> *For every one that does evil **hates the light**,*
> *neither comes to the light,*
> *lest his deeds should be reproved." (Jn 3:19-20)*

Other people can confuse us (2Tim 2:17-18)

How Does God Reveal Himself and Speak to Man?

The Holy Spirit speaks to us in two ways:

First, by '**GENERAL REVELATION**' - revealing **GOD AS CREATOR**

and secondly, '**SPECIAL REVELATION**' - revealing **GOD AS REDEEMER**

1. "GENERAL REVELATION" - GOD AS CREATOR
'General Revelation' is the **knowledge of God through creation or nature**

...and is called "**Natural Theology**" or "**God Consciousness**"

"Because that which may be known of God is
manifest in them*;*
*For **God hath showed it unto them**.*
*For the invisible things of him from the **creation** of the world are*
clearly seen*, being understood*
by the things that are made
Even His eternal power and Godhead:
so that they are without excuse..."
(Rom 1:19-20)

The Bible teaches that **all mankind can know enough about God through 'GENERAL REVELATION'** to believe, reach out and seek Him...

This knowledge comes through our **"CONSCIENCE"** - *"God has SHOWN IT TO THEM" (Rom 1:19)*

*"For when the **Gentiles**, which have not the law,*
do by nature the things contained in the law*,*
these, having not the law, are a law unto themselves:
*Which **show the work of the law written in their hearts**,*
*their **conscience** also **bearing witness**,*
*and their **thoughts** the mean while*
accusing *or else* **excusing** *one another." (Rom 2:14-15)*

The use of the word **"NATURE"** is referring to the fact that it is **NATURAL for us to know God.**

**We know by what is 'NATURAL TO US'
what is right and wrong, good and evil**

Paul also uses the word **"CONSCIENCE"** revealing that we are **'FREE MORAL BEINGS'**, **knowing right and wrong.**

The use of the word **"THOUGHTS"** is also significant

because **we are gifted** by God **with 'INTELLECT' to work this out!**

b. **"OBSERVATION"** - *"(God) from the creation of the world ARE CLEARLY SEEN" (Rom 1:20)*

> *"Nevertheless he left not himself without **witness**,*
> *in that He did **good**, and gave us **rain** from heaven,*
> *and **fruitful seasons**, filling our hearts with **food** and*
> ***gladness**." (Acts 14:17)*

> *"That they should seek the Lord,*
> *if haply they might feel after Him, and find Him,*
> ***though He be not far from every one of us**:*
> *For **in him we live, and move, and have our being**;*
> *as certain also of your own poets have said,*
> *For we are also his offspring." (Acts 17:27-28)*

"Creation is the finger print of God"

Last of all Paul concludes that we can know about God from our **"HISTORY"** - *"When they knew God" (Rom 1:21)*

> *"Because that, **when they knew God**,*
> ***they glorified Him not as God, neither were***
> ***thankful;***
> *but became vain in their imaginations,*
> *and their foolish heart was darkened." (Rom 1:21)*

2. "SPECIAL REVELATION" - GOD AS REDEEMER

'Special Revelation' is the **knowledge of God through the Biblical Revelation of the Lord Jesus Christ which** is a **superior** and **clearer communication** by God to man.

'Special Revelation' **began in the Old Testament** and **culminated as His ultimate communication in the**

Lord Jesus Christ through the "Living Word made flesh"

"Long ago God spoke to the fathers by the prophets
at different times and in different ways.
In these last days,
He has spoken to us by [His] Son.
God has appointed Him heir of all things and made the
universe through Him.
The Son is the radiance of God's glory
and the exact expression of His nature,
sustaining all things by His powerful word." (Heb 1:1-3)

The conveying of "Special Revelation"

a. "The Bible" - The Written Word Of God

"But He answered and said, 'It is written,
Man shall not live by bread alone,
*but by **every word that proceeds out of the mouth***
***of God**.'" (Matt 4:4)*

Being born again, not of corruptible seed,
but of incorruptible,
*by the **word of God**, which lives and abides for ever.*
For all flesh is as grass, and all the glory of
man as the flower of grass.
The grass withers, and the flower thereof falls away:
*But the **word of the Lord endures forever**.*
*And **this is the word which by the gospel is***
***preached unto you**." (1Pet 1:23-25)*

b. "A Variety Of Communications"

"Long ago God spoke to the fathers by the prophets
*at **different times** and in **different ways**..." (Heb 1:1)*

God spoke directly and personally to Adam and Eve and through visions, dreams and angelic appearances to the patriarchs and the prophets. He also spoke with extra-ordinary communications at different times through objects such as the "burning bush", the "voice out of Cloud" and even a donkey.

c. "God's Ultimate Communication" - The Lord Jesus Christ

> *"Has in these **last days spoken unto us by His Son**,*
> *whom He hath appointed heir of all things,*
> *by whom also He made the worlds;*
> *Who **being the brightness of His glory**,*
> *and the express image of His person,*
> *and upholding all things by the word of His power,*
> *when He had by Himself purged our sins,*
> *sat down on the right hand of the Majesty on high."*
> *(Heb 1:2-3)*

> *"Who is the **image** of the **invisible God**,*
> *the firstborn of every creature." (Col 1:15)*

All of these communications have culminated and climaxed in the clearest way through the person of The Lord Jesus Christ, who spoke in person while on earth and continues to speak through His Word and the Holy Spirit.

The Holy Spirit continues the work of revealing and glorifying Christ.

d. "The Ongoing Work Of The Holy Spirit"

The Holy Spirit has been God's most **frequent agent of communication** with man.
The primary work of the Holy Spirit is '**REVEALER**'.

The Holy Spirit...

i.   **Reveals** Truth
ii.   **Testifies** of Christ
iii. **Leads** and **Guides**
iv.   **Convicts** and **Convinces**
v.   **Reveals God** through **supernatural** miracles and signs

---

WHEN THE 'REVEALER' VISITS US
WE CAN SEE AND HEAR GOD... EVERYWHERE!

"For this people's heart is waxed gross,
*and their ears are **dull of hearing**,*
*and their **eyes they have closed**;*
*lest at any time they should **see** with their eyes,*
*and **hear** with their ears,*
*and should **understand** with their heart, and should be*
***converted**,*
*and I should **heal** them.*
But blessed are your eyes, for they see:
***and your ears, for they hear.** (Matt 13:15-16)*

*"For you **were** once **darkness**,*
*but now you **are light** in the Lord:*
walk as children of light." (Eph 5:8)

*"Who has **delivered** us from the **power of darkness**,*
*and has **translated** us **into the kingdom of his dear***
***Son**." (Col 1:13)*

*"The **eyes of your understanding being***
***enlightened**;*
*that you may **know** what is the hope of his calling,*
and what the riches of the glory of his
inheritance in the saints,
And what is the exceeding greatness of his

power toward us who believe,
according to the working of his mighty power."
(Eph 1:18-19)

CHAPTER EIGHT

When the Holy Spirit Comes to Stay

Whenever the Holy Spirit encounters man, something gives...and it is never the Holy Spirit!!

The Holy Spirit is God, therefore He is sovereign.

The Holy Spirit is independent of human understanding, convention, mentality and opinion.

> *"For My thoughts are not your thoughts,*
> *neither are your ways My ways,*
> *declares the Lord.*
> *For as the heavens are higher than the earth,*
> *So are My ways higher than your ways*
> *And My thoughts than your thoughts "*
> *(Is 55:8-9)*

The Holy Spirit is on a mission...**to glorify Christ on the earth and bring all men to salvation**.

In our post-modern, self indulgent, self orientated and self-pleasing mindset and culture, we are not prepared for the Divine, the unpredictable, the intrusive and miraculous **MOMENTS OF THE HOLY SPIRIT!**

> *"And when the Day of Pentecost arrived,*
> *they were all together in one place.*
> ***AND SUDDENLY THERE CAME FROM HEAVEN***
> *A sound like a mighty rushing wind,*

And it filled the house where they were sitting.
And divided tongues as of fire appeared to them
And rested on each one of them.

*And they were all **FILLED WITH THE HOLY SPIRIT***
AND BEGAN TO SPEAK IN OTHER TONGUES
AS THE SPIRIT GAVE THEM UTTERANCE."
(Acts 2:1-4)

There are usually **FOUR RESPONSES TO 'HOLY SPIRIT MOMENTS':**

1. *"They were **AMAZED AND ASTONISHED.**"* (Acts 2:7)
    'Astonished' = "Astounded, dumbfounded, flabbergasted".

2. *"They were **AMAZED AND PERPLEXED.**"* (Acts 2:12)
    'Perplexed' = "Puzzled, troubled by doubt, mystified and confounded".

3. *"But others **MOCKED**, saying, 'They are drunk.'"* (Acts2:12)
    To 'mock' means, "to treat with scorn or contempt, to ridicule and to make fun of".

4. *"And **FEAR** came upon every soul."* (Acts 2:43)
    'Fear' literally means "terror, horror panic and apprehension."

...and nothing ever changes!

The Bible presents many examples of the Holy Spirit acting counter to human preferences and plans. Here are three examples:

1. Saul, The Murderer, Had A Holy Spirit Moment!
"But Saul, still breathing threats and murder
against the disciples of the Lord
...so that if he found any belonging to the Way, men or women,

he might bring them bound to Jerusalem.
Now as he went on his way, he approached Damascus,
AND SUDDENLY A LIGHT FROM HEAVEN
FLASHED AROUND HIM.
And falling to the ground he heard a voice saying to him,
"Saul, Saul, why are you persecuting Me?" (Acts 9:1-4)

God interrupted Paul's plans, his journey, his purpose, his life!

...AND GOD WILL DO THE SAME WITH YOU AND ME!

We should not think for a moment that God is subject to our personal preferences, convenience, comfort and rights to individual autonomy.

When God decides it is the right moment He will turn up, act in our circumstances and **EVERYTHING WILL CHANGE!**

ONE HOLY SPIRIT MOMENT
IS A LIFE TRANSFORMING MOMENT

---

2. Peter, The Great 'Apostle To The Jews', Had A Holy Spirit Moment!

"Peter went on the housetop about the sixth hour to pray.
And he became hungry and wanted something to eat,
But while they were preparing it,
HE FELL INTO A TRANCE
And saw the heavens opened and something like a great sheet descending,
Being let down by its four corners upon the earth." (Acts 10:9-11)

The setting and significance of this moment is important to understand.

The apostles were living in direct disobedience to the command of the Lord Jesus Christ:

> *"**GO** therefore and make disciples of **ALL NATIONS!**"*
> *(Matt 28:19)*

Peter and the other apostles, however, remained based in Jerusalem and were stuck in their Jewish culture only preaching the gospel to Jews.

> *"Now those who were scattered abroad*
> *because of the persecution that arose over Stephen*
> *travelled as far as Phoenicia and Cyprus and Antioch,*
> ***SPEAKING THE WORD TO NO ONE EXCEPT***
> ***JEWS.*** *"(Acts 11:19)*

But when the Holy Spirit decided it was time to change and reach the Gentiles, Peter had no choice, the Holy Spirit moved!

3. Barnabas, 'The Son Of Encouragement', Had A Holy Spirit Moment!

> *"The report of this came to the ears of the church in Jerusalem,*
> ***AND THEY SENT BARNABAS TO ANTIOCH.***
> *When he came and saw the grace of God,*
> *He was glad, and he exhorted them all to remain*
> *faithful to the Lord,*
> *For he was a good man, full of the Holy Spirit and of faith.*
> *And a great many people were added to the Lord."*
> *(Acts 11:22-24)*

Barnabas was happy encouraging the church at Jerusalem. He had no aspirations or plans for anything else…**UNTIL HE HAD A HOLY SPIRIT MOMENT!**

…AND EVERYTHING CHANGED FROM THAT MOMENT!

As a result, Barnabas found himself in the centre of a major move of God, leading and raising up the greatest apostle of all, Paul.

WE ALL NEED THE HOLY SPIRIT
TO MOVE UPON US
TO SAVE US, FILL US, RENEW US... AND CHANGE
THE WAY WE ARE LIVING!

"And we all, with unveiled face,
beholding the glory of the Lord,
are BEING TRANSFORMED
into the same image
FROM ONE DEGREE OF GLORY TO ANOTHER.

"FOR THIS COMES FROM THE LORD
WHO IS THE SPIRIT." (2Cor 3:18)

CHAPTER NINE

The Holy Spirit: The Wild Goose

"The wind blows where it wants to,
and you hear the sound thereof,
but cannot tell from where it comes,
and where it goes:
so is every one that is born of the Spirit."
(Jn 3:8)

Have you ever considered the commonly accepted symbol of the Holy Spirit: the gentle, white, domesticated, 'farm-yard' dove.

Have you ever wondered, like me, why this symbol of the Holy Spirit doesn't seem to fit in with the actual nature and actions of the Holy Spirit in the New Testament and throughout the revivals of history?

The Holy Spirit was there from the commencement of Jesus' ministry, suddenly and unexpectantly appearing and landing on Him at the River Jordan, with John the Baptist declaring;

"And John bare record, saying,
*I saw the Spirit descending from heaven **like a dove (pigeon)**,*
and it abode upon Him. And I knew Him not:
but He that sent me to baptise with water,
the same said to me,
Upon whom you see the Spirit descending, and remaining on Him,
this is He who baptizes with the Holy Spirit." (Jn 1:32-33)

What 'dove' was John the Baptist referring to?

Over the centuries the Romanized state church has presented the Holy Spirit as a tamed, gentle, predictable, and controllable, farm-yard dove. But is this what John saw?

The 'dove' that John the Baptist saw would have been a wild, rock pigeon; a bird commonly found in the wilderness desert of Palestine. These were the wild birds that followed the winds in search of food and water. They have always been seen as the symbol of 'the messenger'.

The Wild Goose: The Celtic Christian symbol of the Holy Spirit

The Celtic Christians of Ireland and Scotland received their understanding of the Holy Spirit directly from the apostles Andrew and John and Paul from Galatia and the 'desert fathers' of the Bible lands.

When they combined this knowledge with their personal experiences of the Holy Spirit, they chose their native Wild Goose to be the symbol of the Holy Spirit.

How different this is from the 'official symbol' that has pervaded the western church for nearly 2000 years.

The Holy Spirit is a 'Wild Goose'

Every move of God throughout church history, and especially the Pentecostal revivals of this century, have been more like 'wild goose' experiences than 'gentle dove' experiences!

Religion, no matter what brand, always reduces God to a concept, a sanitized and civilized form that fits neatly into its way of thinking without causing too much disruption. But this is not the way it is with the Holy Spirit!

The Holy Spirit is sovereign, free and unpredictable!

Exploding the Myth: 'The Holy Spirit is a gentleman'

It is a widely accepted view in Christendom today that 'the Holy Spirit is a gentleman', but this couldn't be further from the truth.

The Holy Spirit is gentle and kind, yes, but 'civilized'? No!

The notion that Christ represents a polite, civilized and controlled religion is a man-made fabrication, reducing God to a human idea.

When Jesus, consumed by the Holy Spirit's zeal for God's House, took scourges and drove out the money changers from the temple; He was not acting very 'gentlemanly'.

When Jesus constantly embarrassed the Pharisees in public by calling them "a den of snakes" (Matt 23:33), he was not 'gentlemanly', or 'civilized'.

Yet Jesus was always gentle towards every sinner repenting.

When the Holy Spirit moves, we must respond and go with Him

When the moment comes for God's will to happen, the Holy Spirit acts suddenly and sovereignly with little regard for the rules and regulations of religious protocol.

The apostle Peter learned this as he went about ministry for God in his own way, when suddenly the Holy Spirit struck him down in a trance and presented him with a sheet filled with all kinds of non-kosher food.

Yes Holy Spirit

> *"And there came a voice to him,*
> *Rise, Peter; kill, and eat. But Peter said, Not so, Lord;*
> *for I have never eaten any thing that is common or unclean." (Acts*
> *10:13-14)*

"Not so, Lord?" What do you mean Peter? What are you saying?

Peter was blinded by his religious conscience, culture and ideas. He couldn't see how 'unclean Gentiles' could receive the Grace of God. So he argues with God three times; "Not so, Lord?"

It was time for God to move on the Gentiles but Peter had problems with that idea.

The Holy Spirit's interaction with Peter revealed that He had no regard for Jewish (or any other religious) sensitivities, traditions or restrictions.

The Holy Spirit moved sovereignly without Peter's agreement.

When the Holy Spirit moves, we must respond and go with Him! No matter who we are, what we are, or where we are!

The Holy Spirit graciously repeated the vision to Peter three times, and concluded emphatically with the statement:

> **"What God has cleansed you must not call**
> **common (unclean)!"** *(Acts 10:15)*

To Peter's credit he came into line and acknowledged God was moving among the Gentiles.
Let the Wild Goose fly!

Wind, fire and the Wild Goose; these are the 'untameable

symbols' of the Holy Spirit.

We can all allow the Holy Spirit to be free in our lives. All we need do is invite Him

"YES, HOLY SPIRIT!"

Prayer of Invitation
to the Wild Goose of the Holy Spirit

*Blessed Holy Spirit of God
I invite you now
To lead me into
God's exciting plan for my life.*

I throw off every man-made restriction of You.

*As the Wild Goose of God,
I open myself to Your freedom, wildness and creativity,
I receive You now*

*In the Name of Jesus Christ.
AMEN*

CHAPTER TEN

"How To Receive The Holy Spirit"

There are some basic prerequisites to receiving the Holy Spirit:

1. We must be 'BORN AGAIN' – this is a gift and experience only for those who have experienced the new birth.

> *"Have you* **RECEIVED** *the Holy Spirit*
> **SINCE YOU BELIEVED***?" (Acts 19:2)*

2. We must ask in FAITH – there must be an operation of trust and belief in the goodness and love of God.

> *"If you being evil, know how to give good*
> *gifts to your children,*
> *how much more will your Father in heaven*
> **give the Holy Spirit to them that ask Him***?" (Matt 7:11)*

3. We must be SPIRITUALLY HUNGRY – God is always looking for a hungry and thirsty heart that is seeking for spiritual realities.

> *"Blessed are those who* **hunger** *and* **thirst** *for*
> *righteousness for they will be* **filled**." *(Matt 5:6)*

4. We must be OPEN AND YIELDED TO GOD – a resistant attitude is a blockage to spiritual experience.

*"And **grieve not the Holy Spirit of God…**" (Eph 4:30)*

5. We must have the capacity to 'DRINK' – we know how to drink when we are truly thirsty!

*"If anyone is thirsty he should come to Me and **drink**…*
*He said this about the **Spirit**, whom those who believed in Him were going to receive." (Jn 7:37-39)*

Prayer to Receive the Holy Spirit

Lord Jesus,
I ask you to give me the Gift of Your Holy Spirit
Please fill me with your Holy Spirit and His power
So I can live an empowered life for You
Holy Spirit, I now receive You into my life
AMEN

What can I expect to happen?

When we ask God for anything we are to believe that He not only hears us but will also answer our prayers.

*"And this is the **confidence** that we have in Him,*
*that, if we ask any thing according to His will, **He hears us**:*
And if we know that He hears us, whatever we ask,
***we know that we have** the petitions (prayers) that we desired of Him." (1Jn 5:14-15)*

And so, when we ask for the Holy Spirit we can be confident that we will receive the Holy Spirit, just as God promised in His Word.

"If you then, being evil,
know how to give good gifts to your children:
how much more will your heavenly Father
***give the Holy Spirit to them that ask him?"** (Lk 11:13)*

When the Holy Spirit comes, you can expect anything to happen.

You may experience a quiet, overwhelming calm and peaceful feeling deep within your heart. Or, maybe a more physical, outward experience like some people who shake and even fall down on the ground.

We all react differently to the power of the Holy Spirit.

So, whatever happens, it is important to relax and trust God that this is a good and perfect gift from Him. Therefore, receive the Holy Spirit with an open and believing heart.

> *"**Every good gift and every perfect gift is from above**,*
> *and comes down from the **Father** of lights..." (Jas 1:17)*

Will I begin to Speak in another language ("Speaking in Tongues")?

Most people we pray for begin to speak in a foreign language as soon as the Holy Spirit fills them. Others experience this later.

If you don't experience this immediately, don't worry. As you continue to receive prayer and trust the Holy Spirit, He will complete His work in you.

> *"And they were all filled with the Holy Spirit,*
> *and began to speak with other tongues (languages),*
> *as the Spirit gave them utterance (the ability)." (Acts 2:4)*

BIBLIOGRAPHY

Strongs Exhaustive Concordance, Compact Edition, James Strong, Baker Book House, Grand Rapids, Michigan, USA, 1977.

Vines Expository Dictionary of New Testament Words, Oliphants Ltd, USA, 1940.

Greek-English Lexicon of the New Testament, Joseph H. Thayer, Zondervan, USA.